GLITZCH! USA

written by

High Pellet
Hugh Kellett

published by

Bend Facts
Bene Factum

BFP

Hugh Kellett studied languages at Oxford and has been playing around with words in London advertising agencies most of his life. Starting his career in the heady days of the 70s at an American multi-national in London, he has been involved with TV, press, radio, poster and social media campaigns in many sectors from beer to beauty, food to financial, technology to travel, and pretty much everything in between. He has dealt with the foibles of government ministers and celebrity hairdressers in the UK, and spun the fables of Wall Street bankers and detergent salesmen in the US, representing them all in the noble art of myth-making and marketing manipulation, most recently at the London offices of the international giant Publicis.

Changes to the way we communicate with each other, the increasing role of technology in driving those changes and the startling unforeseen side effects of that technology, all struck him as worthy of the deep and serious study you have before you....read on.

Glitzch! USA

Published in 2013 by
Bene Factum Publishing Ltd
PO Box 58122
London SW8 5WZ

Email: inquiries@bene-factum.co.uk
www.bene-factum.co.uk

ISBN: 978-1-909657-22-9

Text © Hugh Kellett

The rights of Hugh Kellett to be identified as the Author of this Work have been asserted by him in accordance with the Copyright, Designs and Patents Act, 1988.

All rights reserved. This book is sold under the condition that no part of it may be reproduced, copied, stored in a retrieval system or transmitted in any form or by any means, electronic, mechanical, photocopying, recording or otherwise without prior permission in writing of the publisher.

A CIP catalogue record of this is available from the British Library.

Cover, illustrations and book design by Tony Hannaford.

Printed in China on behalf of Latitude Press.

To my daring wife

All tights reversed

All rights reserved

The Joy of Text

It was a day like any other and I was on a train home texting a friend, my mind elsewhere. It was no more than a two liner. I hit the send button before leaning back in my seat to watch the familiar English landscape fly past. Five minutes later the incoming message signal bleeped and I opened the reply. My friend was nonplussed...What did I mean by the text? In fact, WHAT THE HELL did I mean by the text?

Checking my original I saw what he meant – it was seriously rude. The predictive messaging facility had (once again) caught me out, and I had sent a text whose meaning bore scant relation to its original intent. Everyone has made this mistake at some time but the thought occurred to me that, with our lives being increasingly controlled by machines, predictive software might have been infiltrated by a mischievous little gremlin that manipulated our words for its own edification. There was a bug in the system and it was buggering things up. Literally.

Had the great technology and communication corporations that permeate our lives at every level unwittingly unleashed – for the sake of speed and spelling convenience – a rogue force that was spreading with virus-like alacrity, voraciously mutating the building blocks of civilisation – words? Destabilising things. Was it unwitting? Had the CIA got something to do with it? Or the Russians (the gremlin from the Kremlin)?

Delving further into the fantastical, I started experimenting with the range of possible options my device was suggesting on screen as I built a word. Choose the "wrong" predictive suggestion* and you can be taken off on a demented, but, as I discovered, often worryingly informative, journey by this little monster. A strange process of illumination. It seemed that the gremlin was indeed actively delivering messages and insights from another plane, via a sort of hilarious poltergeisting of language. In many instances and when the mood took it, its messages seemed to cast a light on some things and on others a shadow.

Mischievously, mockingly, maddeningly, it seemed to have it in for us. Nothing and no-one seemed safe from its impishly revisionist bile.

The result? The subversion of things we know and a questioning of things we hold to be true – from religion to the law, from politics to language and literature, from sport to social, and dammit, right down to American history itself. We were being relentlessly and scurrilously undermined. So if, in the pages that follow, the gremlin causes shock and outrage, please remember, Dear Reader, that I am merely a messenger, or at best a medium.

As a consequence of that wayward text, *Glitzch!* was born. Whether the gremlin be malicious or merely mischievous, let alone mildly miraculous, is for the reader to decide. The examples on the following pages are genuine possibilities. Sorry, I'll rephrase that: "The examiner on the flowing pageboy ate penguins possibly". You get the idea. Next time you text, tweet or type – remember the gremlin itching to be heard, to voice what we're loath to say and go where we fear to tread.

The original version of *Glitzch!* was published in the UK, where I allowed the gremlin to take an impish swipe at the great story of Britain and the noble institutions that I knew so well. I was tickled to do the same for other countries, and since I knew little of America, and the educational system here doesn't teach American history beyond jokes about Little Big Horn, I researched the origins of the US and embarked on a voyage of discovery that proved as full of havoc as its British counterpart.

---

*All clear? Thought not. A fuller explanation for the more forensic or technically minded is on page 154.

Health Warning

This book has two inherent problems.
The first is that it is written by a Limey.
The second is that it is not for the easily offended.
Had it appeared 25 years ago, the first point in history when it could technically have been written, it would have provoked deep moral outrage from Pennsylvania to Palm Beach. It could still be an affront to many people even in our more tolerant times and is seriously rude in some parts. It mentions parts of the body, and dwells somewhat on those other two subjects that should not be raised at dinner parties – politics and religion.
DO NOT READ ON IF YOU THINK YOU MIGHT TAKE OFFENCE.
Don't even turn the page.

Oh, all right, go on then…

First let me testify to one critical fact.

This is the United States re-stated in predictive text. Every entry has been authentically produced by my cell phone.

So everything in this book must be true.

The Oath

I do silently sweat
that I shall tell the tripe,
the wholehearted tripe and
nothing but the tripe,
so hello my god.

The Oath
I do solemnly swear
that I shall tell the truth,
the whole truth and
nothing but the truth,
so help me God.

America.

Land of the free! Cradle of opportunity!
The world's greatest democracy.
311,591,917 happily co-existing souls.
Policeman of the planet.
Superpower par excellence*.

But you were not always thus.
Only via sweat and toil and general speed with a gun was
this great nation born.

This is your story…America.
The American Dream.
Be proud.
Welcome to…

* French

The Untied States of Africa

The United States of America

So how did you all begin? Well with the…

Ruffians

Russians

...of course, who else?

Millennia ago, some frozen Siberian folk braved the Bering Sea and settled in the North of the great land. They had the vast country to themselves and lived a simple noble life.

Since then, political correctness has played its part in naming these original peoples, and no-one, not even they themselves, quite knows where they stand today.

Are we talking about…

Naïve Poles

Native Peoples

Ingenious Africans

Indigenous Americans

Reserved Individuals

Red Indians

Africans Indisposed

American Indians

Resins

Redskins

Injunctions

Injuns

Here are a few of their better known tribes...

Creeps Crowds Moveable Mexicans Urologists Cheekbones Chryslers	Shahs Conman Chivalrous Solicitors Algorithms
Cree Crow Mohawk Mohican Iroquois Cherokee Cheyenne	Shawnee Comanche Choctaw Sioux Algonquin

The men and women were respectively known as...

Beavers

Braves

Squats

Squaws

...presided over by a headman, who catered for their every need, called a...

Chef

Chief

Which was good because the tribes were partial to massive…

Buffets

Buffalo

So vast was the land, and so full of meat and grain, that
the tribes moved over the great plains and lived in perfect harmony.

However, these peace-loving folk never went to school and were
thus not overly gifted in the defence technology department, never
really progressing from the primitive weapons of their ancestors...

Bowels and Marrows

Bows and arrows

Effective weapon if used downwind. Early form of gas warfare.

…even though they are credited (alas too late) with inventing the…

Tomato Missile

Tomahawk Missile

Peach Helicopter

Apache Helicopter

…and of course the…

Tomtom

Meanwhile, over in Europe, we are talking 500 years ago, folks had been studying hard. With study came knowledge, and with knowledge greed.

Consumed with a particular greed were the men in tight pants from the Mediterranean, who sailed over the horizon. Most notably two friendly fellows…

Christine Columnist

Christopher Columbus

And the one who endowed the US with your name…

Amerigo Vespucci

...otherwise you might have become the drugs centre, sorry center, of the world and be called Colombia.

But it was us Brits, with our evil Queen Elizabeth* in the late 1500s who did most to disrupt the peaceful life of the native Americans, and sent men of war westward in search of the New World. Elizabeth had come from a long line of partial inbreds called the Royal Family. This led them to be unpredictable, irascible and prone to wearing large cod pieces.**

The very worst of these guys, as we shall see, was the extra-mad tax tyrant King of England of German extraction...

---

* Not the current one.

** Not something you get from McDonald's on a Friday but an embroidered appendage, worn on the outside over a man's, er, appendage, so that he doesn't have to take his tights off*** when he needs to use his appendage for something. As an aside, the item was named after the old English word for scrotum – the cod – not as a euphemism for the thing dangling or sticking out above it. Which was smellier in late medieval times – a cod piece or a piece of cod – is a matter of keen conjecture amongst historical scholars. As a further aside, because I know this interests you, the general rule was that the larger the cod piece the smaller its contents. This is a tradition that I understand continues to this day in America with "small" men driving big automobiles.

*** Superman presumably had this problem.

Grotesque the Thin

George the Third

America belongs to us

George will be remembered forever by the Brits as the guy who scandalously lost our valuable American colonies.

Because you're interested, and for those of you not attending school, here is a quick one-page history refresher of some of the key British regal folk…

Some of the Brutish Totalitarian Family

Some of the British Royal Family

William the Conjuror
Ricky the Loony
Ricky the Sexy
Henry the Filth
Edward the Gout
Richard the Thick
Kind Henry the Either
Jamaican the Fist
Charming the Filch
Grotesque the Thin
Wilt the Foul
Queer Vicar

Well, it's either you or you I shall wed, or it could be you, you or you.

William the Conqueror
Richard the Lionheart
Richard the Second
Henry the Fifth
Edward the Fourth
Richard the Third
King Henry the Eighth
James the First
Charles the First
George the First
William the Fourth
Queen Victoria

We are not abusive

We are not amused

Yee hah… The big loser in all this →

There, part of the unbroken line stretching back in time. Reassuring, eh?

Do Americans sometimes miss not having a Royal Family in the US?

Are they occasionally not just a little green with envy?

King George of England wasn't that bad a guy really, was he?

Because, in dumping the monarchy America also forfeited the *nobility*, that critical substructure that supports it, so no American could have one of these fancy titles in front of his name…

The Inability

Duck
Marquee
Ear
Discount
Bacon
Hardness
Bayonet
Knife
Dane

Order of impotence

Order of importance

The Nobility
Duke
Marquess
Earl
Viscount
Baron
Baroness
Baronet
Knight
Dame

Still, there were ways round this – you got Duke Ellington and Count Basie. Not to mention your crowning glory, Martin Luther King.

So on balance you probably did OK out of it in the end.

But we digress…

Back to Italy, late 1500s.

The Brits' arch enemy was plotting how he might satisfy his lust for ground in God's name and had sent spies and explorers to your shores. This was of course none other than the leader of the orthodox Church, well known for his zealous, some would say, inquisitive*, indeed red hot pursuit of godliness…

*The Inquisition held about 49,000 trials.

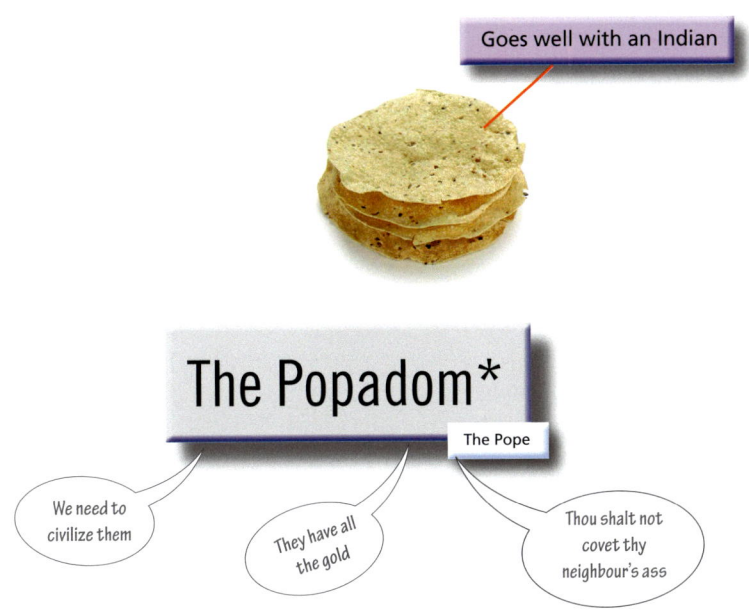

* Religious wars were a major limiting factor on the population, the European 30 Years War alone accounting for a deficit of over 11,000,000 people.

Fortunately the Brits, who had broken away from the Church of Rome following a series of disagreements over Henry VIII's pre-nups, had other ideas, and got there first. Otherwise you would be speaking even more Spanish and Italian* than you currently do.

The key organiser was a well known Elizabethan explorer, he of the cloak-over-the-puddle story, and someone who almost certainly explored secret parts of Queen Elizabeth herself…

* As a matter of historical fact, German very nearly became the official tongue of the USA. Imagine.

Sir Waiter Takeaway

Sir Walter Raleigh

What ho, I'm feeling a little ruff today

Sir Walter was actually an unlucky chap, beheaded late in life (or more accurately at the end of his life) for *only* discovering potato and tobacco in the New World and bringing them back to England.

This was particularly unjust when one considers these two commodities make up the staple diet of 95% of Brits today.

The early settlers began arriving, exhausted after the rough Atlantic crossing. They were greasy, stinky, hardy and hairy.

And that was just the women.*

One of the brave Brits, John Smith, fell in love with a beautiful Indian princess, who famously saved him from being beheaded...

* (An oldie but goodie)

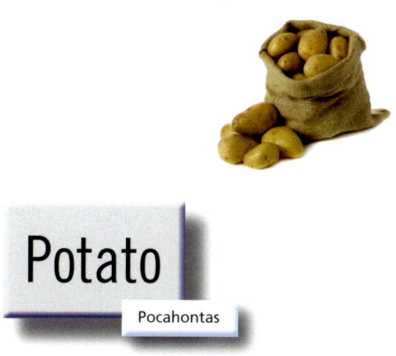

Potato
Pocahontas

It was the first example of multi-culturalism in America. Broadmindedness of this sort was characteristic of the locals, a notable example of being conspicuously ahead of his time was this fellow…

Openly alternative behaviour of this kind attracted a certain section of the British public, and gaily dressed gentlemen adventurers arrived. Via almost entirely peaceful means they persuaded the friendly locals to share their land…

The Brits quite quickly established a strong footing and defended their new shores.

The Mediterranean guys in tights were largely repulsed from the mainland and set up shop in the balmy Atlantic islands and the whole of South America, which better suited their temperament. Here they managed to destroy several ancient civilisations including…

The Antics
The Aztecs

The Incapables
The Incas

Could the British do the same for those pesky North American Indians, who just wouldn't go quietly, as the pale faces moved inexorably West?

Meanwhile, the crafty French had shown an interest too, to annoy the Brits, and had joined in manoeuvres and bagged Canada in the North.

It was all set up for a superbowl style showdown: the nations and faiths that had been fighting each other for centuries in Europe were about to play an away game, known variously as the French Indian War or…

The Semen Test War

The Seven Years War

The Brits were in a strong position as they were a nation of seamen

…which the British fought against a coalition that rather reflected national characteristics…

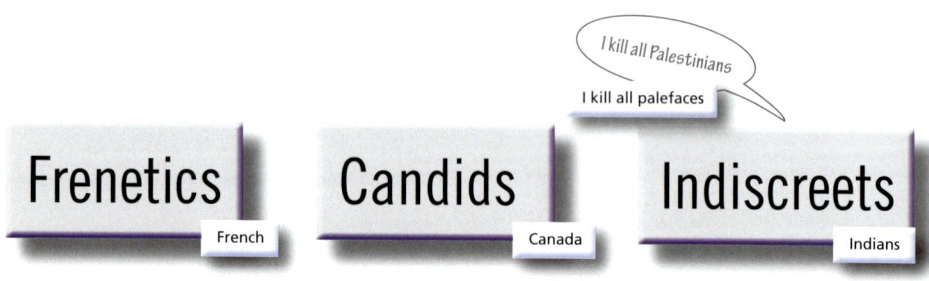

Frenetics

French

Candids

Canada

I kill all Palestinians

I kill all palefaces

Indiscreets

Indians

The insane King George of England, bled dry by the cost of the war, was imposing very high taxes on his subjects in the new colonies.

Just like today, they sought ways to circumvent the taxman and the cry went up…

"No vacation without representatives"

"No taxation without representation"

Revolution was in the air.

To start the whole thing off there was a major social gathering, the…

...followed by the full outbreak of the…

*An early version of Rear of the Year.

War of Indecency

War of Independence

This was a serious flash point, but after a long struggle we Brits were blown back where we belonged, all ties with the old country were cut (including the old school tie) and the US of A burst onto the world stage via…

The Declaration of Dependency

The Declaration of Independence

This problem was finally cracked many years later when you introduced...

Inhibition

Prohibition

Wicked King George was replaced with his namesake and America had its first President…

George Washington

…who put you all on the path to a full and fair democracy…

The US Decoration of Indecency
INSURANCE CONGRESS, July 4, 1776

We hold these trusts to be self-evident that all menials are cheated equally, that they are enjoyed by their realtor with certified Italian tights. That among these are Lifestyle, Liberals and the pursuit of Hippies. That to secure these tights, Internments are institutionalized among Members, depriving the just powders from the convent of the governor.

The US Declaration of Independence
IN CONGRESS, JULY 4, 1776

We hold these truths to be self-evident, that all men are created equal, that they are endowed by their Creator with certain unalienable Rights. That among these are Life, Liberty and the pursuit of Happiness. That to secure these rights, Governments are instituted among Men, deriving their just powers from the consent of the governed.

Staying with the theme of undergarments, an important new law was introduced, and America had its first…

…which set out that all people would be dealt with equally under the law…NOT!

Necessary exclusions were included for women, blacks, slaves and of course Indians.

*British English for your more romantic sounding pantyhose.
It is a fact, by the way, that most billionaires are tight.

The key thing was that Americans were (pretty much) all free.

A critical part of this was to allow the newly emancipated population to remain armed and carry…

Gums
Guns

The age old adage of "shoot first, ask questions later" became enshrined in American culture, and a love affair with the gun began.

The most successful was a revolver called…

The Colon
The Colt

...it could blow a man off his feet at twenty paces.

(And, as the cowboys discovered, its performance was enhanced by eating copious amounts of beans.)

Later another even more effective one was invented…

Rattling Fun

Gatling Gun

This weapon could fire 100 rounds in the time it took to arm your tomahawk. It was definitely the future, and only really surpassed in efficacy when, many years later, the jocular theme was maintained with the…

LOL

Comic Bomb

Atomic Bomb

Back to the wild days.

There was the old question of the Indians, and a new even darker issue…

Bravery

Slavery

Slaves were the large number of people who had come in on an enforced package tour from Africa to work the land, for something rather less than the minimum wage.

Particularly in the cotton, sugar and tobacco-rich South they toiled in their white masters'…

Lamentations

Plantations

In 1861, certain of the nation's more liberal leaders in the North, who had few slaves, decided this was iniquitous and old-fashioned, and a terrible war broke out among the good people of America, between the North and the South.

It was known as…

The Civil War

The Considerates
The Confederates

The Unkind
The Union

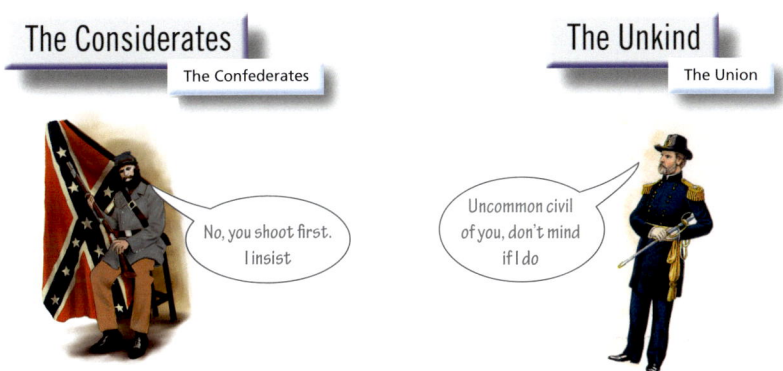

It was so civil that nearly 600,000 people lost their lives.

The winner in the end, by a whisker, was the North, led by…

Abrasive Luncheon

Abraham Lincoln

...abetted by his main General...

Ultra Grand

Ulysses Grant

A new (and quite prescient) patriotic song was introduced...

The Startled Spanked Banker

The Star Spangled Banner

…who would nevertheless fly high…

O'er the land of the feds and the home of the beaver

O'er the land of the free and the home of the brave

As an aside, did you know the tune to this was an original British drinking song. True.

Meanwhile the Indians were STILL on the warpath and there were ongoing battles to try and find a, er, settlement.

Here are some of the key folks involved in the long hours of thrashing out an equitable solution round the table…

Bad Wages
Bald Eagle

Veronica
Geronimo

Spitting Bullets
Sitting Bull

He's got a Big Horn but we'll call it little. It'll certainly be his last stand.

Federal Custody
General Custer

Of the Decent Canary
Of the Seventh Cavalry

In the end the good guys won and the Native Americans found new happiness in specially cordoned-off parts of the country.

The victors had no reservations.

These were the great days of American folklore.

Many household names took to the stage...

Party Garment

Pat Garrett

Wildebeest Bollocks Hillock

Wild Bill Hickok

not to be confused with...

The Warped Brothels

The Earp Brothers

Buff Bollocks

Buffalo Bill

Save Cricket*

Davy Crocket

Jesus James

Jesse James

John Weakly Hardened

John Wesley Hardin

* In this he failed - you took up baseball.

The population grew via immigration as all the outcasts of the world followed our (your?) Founding Fathers and came over here for a bite of the pie.

But, hey, you've always been an accommodating people, known for your tolerance of outsiders, and so you welcomed the whole damn bunch of them...

Groans
Piles
Spots
Dames
Geeks

Germans
Poles
Scots
Danes
Greeks

Irksome
Penis
Stalin
Cheese
Ditch

Irish
Spanish
Italians
Chinese
Dutch

It was a toxic mix and created mayhem.
Everywhere there was…

Shopping
Shooting

Rubbing
Robbing

Banging
Hanging

Whooping
Whipping

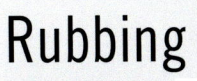

Lashing
Lassoing

Spurting
Spitting

Lunching
Lynching

Panting
Panning

Hairy Breasts
Jail breaks

Synagogues
Dynamite

The government didn't know where the hell all this was leading, and started to ask important questions…

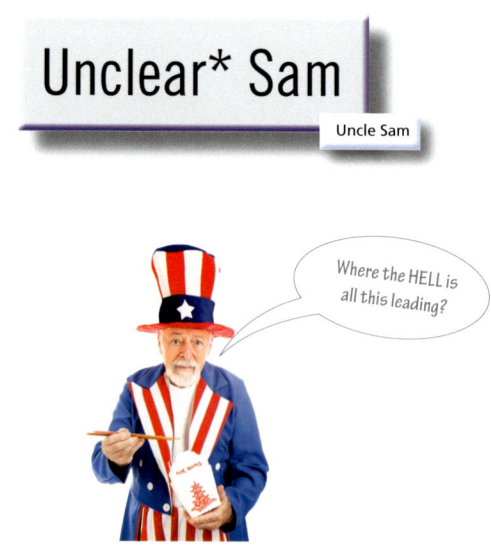

* Note the prophetically anagrammatic possibilities of this word.

But the West was well and truly being opened up and the heady days began, as the good folks of the USA pushed the frontier ever nearer the Pacific.

There was of course a whole lot of banging and shooting, and everyone was after personal expansion, in what was known as the…

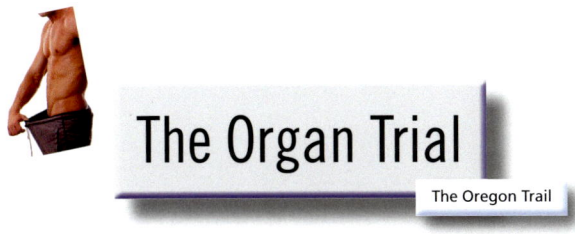

The Oregon Trail

Transport and infrastructure took shape in earnest including the building of…

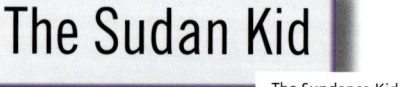

The Unionized Pacifist Tailor

The Union Pacific Railroad

…famously robbed by a couple of apparent foreigners…

Dutch Chassis

Butch Cassidy

…and the early fundamentalist…

The Sudan Kid

The Sundance Kid

The good times started to roll.

The dark days were over, slaves were finally freed and, to cap it all, a major monument was built to enshrine the Land of the Free…

The Statue of Liberty

Overall, things in America were beginning to look pretty swell.

The country was rich in natural resources and in 1888 there was the …

Gold Rush

…and if you hit the big time you made a lucky…

Strike

Talking of golf, in sport you are clearly net contributors, having invented…

Baseness
Baseball

Sucking
Surfing

Numeric Doorbell
American Football

Ten pint howling
Ten Pin bowling

Icecream honey
Ice hockey

Casket
Basketball

Just recently you've taken up our magical national game…

Sorcery
Soccer

At an international level, your sporting prowess lies mainly in…

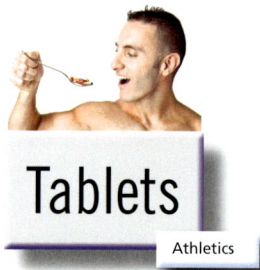

Tablets
Athletics

…which give you staying power when it comes to…

The Long Hump
The Long Jump

…and…

Swinging
Swimming

…both of which can result in a man's…

Pole Fault
Pole vault

Sorry, took a bit of a dog leg there, let's get back onto the fairway of history.

Onto the scene strode folk who thought the pen was mightier than the gun, and wrote about the Deep South, the True North, the Far East and the Mae West, notably your greatest writer…

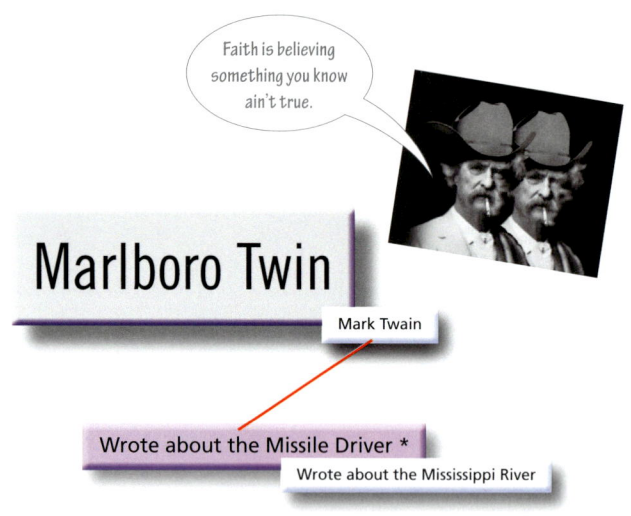

...who made a packet (before it all went up in smoke).

But he had lit the spirit of the American novel and other great writers followed, including...

* Another unhappy prophecy

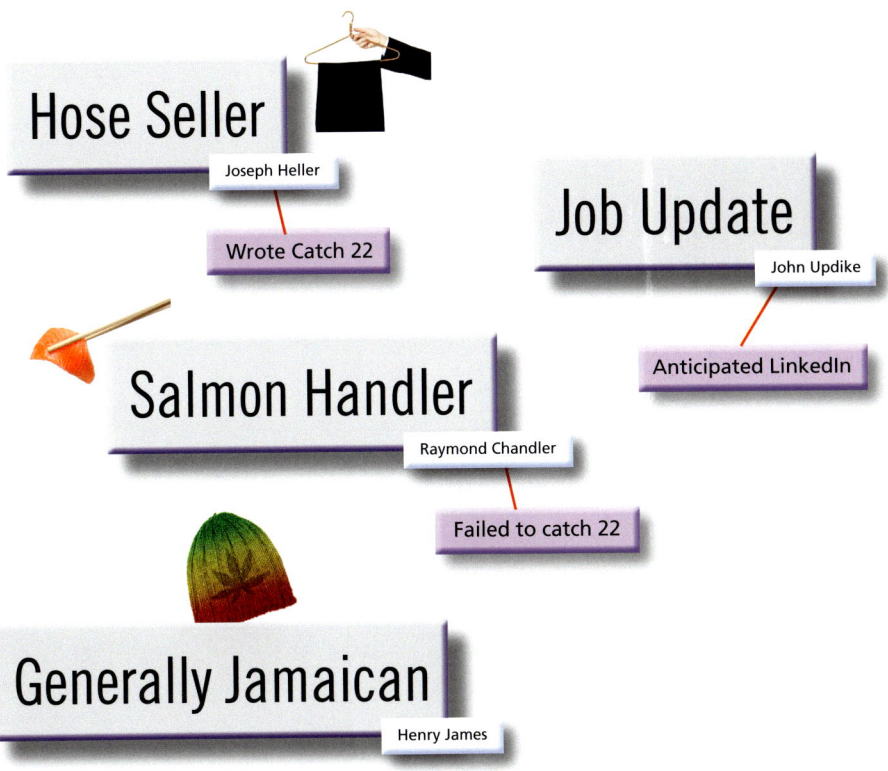

Confusingly this last guy wrote about the

Salesmen Watch Trials

Salem Witch Trials

and

Death of a Salem

Death of a Salesman

Again confusingly, and something that could never happen in prudish Britain, he was married to the most beautiful but ill-fated movie goddess, at least 311 years his junior…

Marilyn Monroe

Individuals all over the country were realising the American dream by inventing things, and many handy items we take for granted today saw the light of day for the first time…

The Hampton
The tampon

Lazarus
Brings a sluggish body back to life
Laxative

Fornication
Formica

Violet Bush
For use afterwards
Toilet brush

Your most prolific inventor was

Thousandth Edition*

Thomas Edison

Contrary to popular folklore, while he had many light bulb moments he did not actually invent the light bulb (a British invention). He was known to have been incandescent about this. His many discoveries included the…

Loving Posture Camera

Moving Picture Camera

> Remember the hanging, dimpled and pregnant chads in the 2000 election?

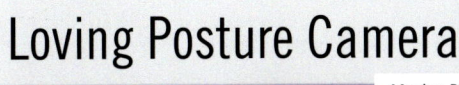

Vote Counterfeiting

Vote Counter

..and with religious zeal he pursued the development of…

Excommunication

Telecommunications

* He registered over 1000 patents.

Critical for transport were the two guys who dieted vigorously to defy gravity, the...

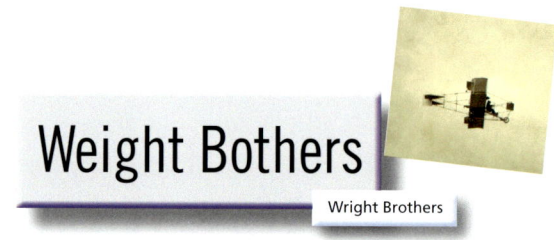

Weight Bothers

Wright Brothers

...and their famous invention...

The Witty Hawaiian

The Kitty Hawk

It was aloha to air travel.

Despite all this progress, racial inequality was still a major issue and it would be many years until the Oval Office was occupied by the best man for the job irrespective of colour.

But a movement called civil rights was gaining traction, immortalised in the words…

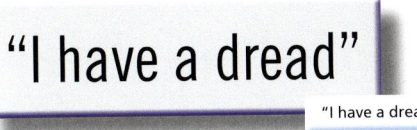

"I have a dream"

One group got very cross about this and objected pointedly…

The Ku Klux Klan

Otherwise religious toleration ruled,
allowing a large number of faiths to practice freely…

Carbohydrates
Suits
Motorists
Bassists
Jehovah's Waitresses
Hormones
Green Orthopaedics
Jewels
Amusements
Creatures
Takers
Buddies
Hindsights

Catholics
Jesuits
Methodists
Baptists
Jehovah's Witnesses
Mormons
Greek Orthodox
Jews
Amish
Creationists
Quakers
Buddhists
Hindus

Pretty well everyone who had a sense of humor seemed to get along just fine.

The US virtues of inventiveness, endeavour, toleration and emancipation, coupled with enormous military might, turned America into the superpower we know today, guardians of the free world.

In the quest for global and domestic peace you developed important new weapons of technology…

Unclear Summaries

Nuclear Submarines

...with a... **Penis**

Periscope

The German Tank

The Sherman Tank

...and more recently the...

The Teaser

The Taser

Funnily enough, it was not always thus. Being mainly peace-loving at heart, you tried to stay out of the global conflicts started by your more quarrelsome European allies.

However, after the scurrilous attack on Pearl Harbour in 1941 by the…

Happiest

Japanese

…you entered the…

Seconded Workers War

Second World War

…and the rest is sushi.

But having started, you had to continue, so you premiered a few more little Eastern wars of your own, most notably one you conducted brilliantly, having waltzed into…

Vienna*

Vietnam

* Considered by many another bad Korea move.

Crack army units were involved including…

The Greek Beers

The Green Berets

The Matinee Corps

The Marine Corps

…who have recently been outdone somewhat in the campaign for global peace by the top secret…

Baby Meals

Navy Seals

Sadly after Vietnam, traditional warfare gradually fell out of fashion as the Russians, your ancestors (see page 14), had whipped up their own...

...so there followed years and years of the...

Cola War

Cold war

Fortunately everyone was protected from ensuing collateral damage by the…

Urine Curtain

Iron curtain

And when that got boring the real dog fight between West and East kicked off, known as the…

War on Terriers

War on Terror

It was a dog eat dog situation. Terriers are one thing but Afghans another breed altogether.

Prior to this, it had always been absolutely tip top critical that America won the…

The Spice Rack

The Space Race

You had the best folk in the world at…

Nasal
NASA

...and did something that was truly out of this world, putting the first...

Man on the moose

Man on the moon

Immortalised as follows...

"One anal stroke for management, one grant less for banking."

"One small step fpr man, one giant leap for mankind."

It was this guy's finest hour…

Richer Nicotine

Richard Nixon

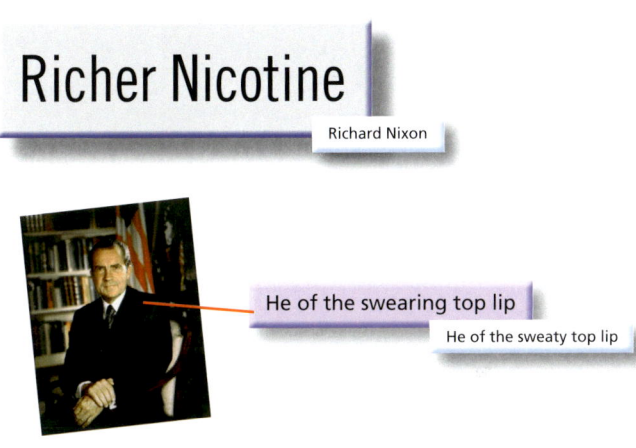

He of the swearing top lip

He of the sweaty top lip

He might sound like a smoker, but he was a healthy guy underneath and will always be mainly remembered for the…

Watermelon Breakfast

Watergate Break-in

Let's have a look at some other notable presidents…

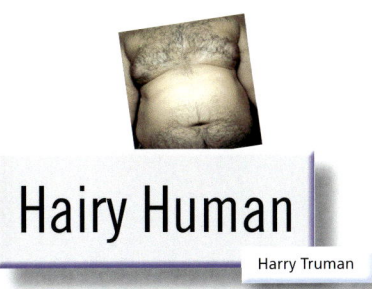

Hairy Human
Harry Truman

Putting it bluntly, placing his head on my body for a cheap joke will probably cause offence.

Frank Rooster
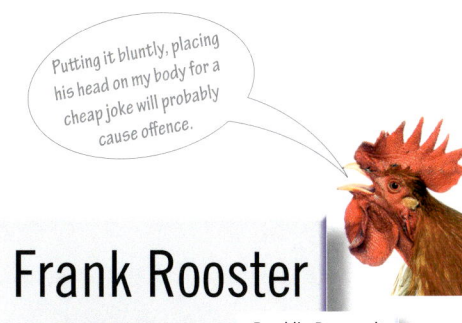

Franklin Roosevelt

Feral Form
Gerald Ford

Bull Clingon
Bill Clinton

Royal Regal
Ronald Regan

Forge Budget x 2
George Bush

…and where they hang out…

Whitewash House

White House

Mongrels
Congress

Capitalist Hilary

Capitol Hill

Sedated

Senate

House of Preventatives

House of Representatives

To protect the homeland and keep the government in power there's a series of uniformed individuals to keep everything ticking...

Cranks in the Polite Force
Orifice
Serpent
Low-level
Cappuccino
Manager
Colon
Insect
Comrade
Supine
Serf

Ranks in the Police Force
Officer
Sergeant
Lieutenant
Captain
Major
Colonel
Inspector
Commander
Superintendent
Sheriff

These guys are backed by several other important undercover organizations…

The Funeral Burial of Investing

The Control Negligence Agency

Notional Guarantors

Federal Bureau of Investigation
The Central Intelligence Agency
The National Guard

Then there's the brave guys and gals on land, sea and air…

Army Cranks
Primate
Corpse
Serf
Warts Official
Fist Low-Level
Decoy Low-Level
Cappuccino
Manager
Half Coloured
Coloured
Brigand Gentry
Manic Gentry

Army Ranks
Private
Corporal
Sergeant
Warrant Officer
First Lieutenant
Second Lieutenant
Captain
Major
Half Colonel
Colonel
Brigadier General
Major General

Navy cranks
Semen
Pet Offering
Chilled Pet Offering
Warts Official
Email
Liechtenstein
Liechtenstein Company
Common
Cappuccino
Rear Admirable
Vices Admirable
Fleshy Admirable

Navy Ranks
Seaman
Petty Officer
Chief Petty Officer
Warrant Office
Ensign
Lieutenant
Lieutenant Commander
Commander
Captain
Rear Admiral
Vice Admiral
Fleet Admiral

Air Force cranks

(in as far as they differ from Army)

Barman
Stiff Serf
Waste Serf

Air Force Ranks
Airman
Staff Sergeant
Master Sergeant

These guys with guns are only let loose when "intelligence" is totally, 100%, completely and unambiguously incontrovertible that national security is at stake.

Most recently this occurred when everyone knew for sure that…

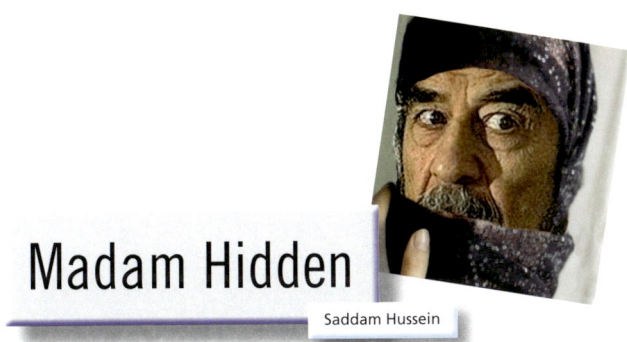

Saddam Hussein

…had…

Wagons of massage instructions

Weapons of mass destruction

I'm likely to go off in 45 minutes

We – and here I proudly mean the US and the UK joined at the hip as allies – certainly weren't going to take that sort of threat lying down (particularly not without oil)

Here's some of the leading guys (and a few of the ladies) in politics we come across in the UK media…

Salary Clinging
Muttering Money
Nose Widen
Safari Pain
Suck Cheese

Hilary Clinton
Mitt Romney
Joseph Biden
Sarah Palin
Dick Cheney

Jog Merry
Beer Ginger
Alarm Greenland
Danish Quayside
Fondle Dice

John Kerry
Newt Gingrich
Alan Greenspan
Dan Quayle
Condoleezza Rice

And the diplomatic great-grandaddy of them all…

Hebrew Messenger

Henry Kissinger

How do they get to the top?

Well, every four years there's this event that most people look forward to, but many women, and some men, dread…

A Residential Erection
A Presidential Election

It's a stiff test and many eventual leaders turn out to be dysfunctional.

It's always a good, clean two-way fight…

Reptilians
Republicans

versus

Demons
Democrats

An aside: The total amount of advertising and promotion spent on US electioneering is estimated at $6 billion. More than the GDP of some African states.

The current incumbent is a decent Democrat and of course needs no introduction…

Black Observer

Barack Obama

Here's some of his counterparts, your loyal allies in Europe…

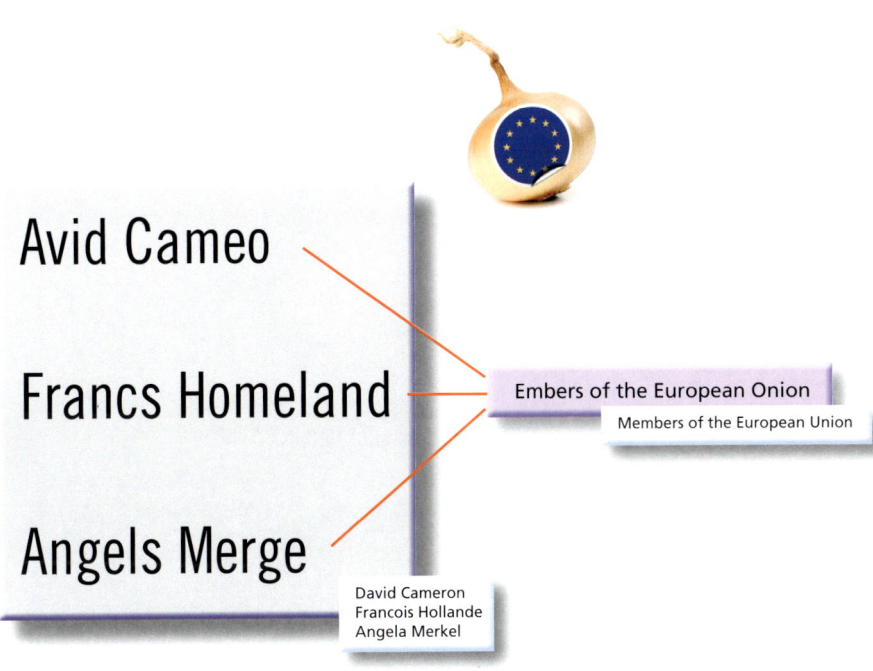

The US government is run by an inner body,
all singing and dancing, called the…

Everything is carefully orchestrated into departments…

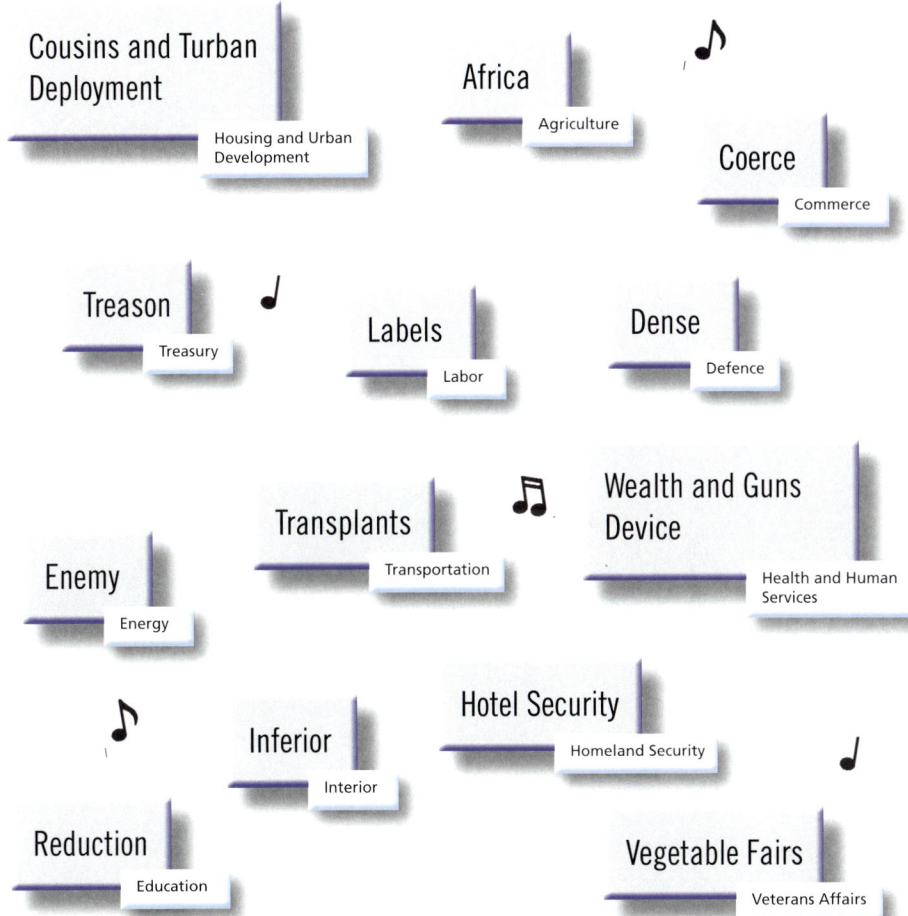

The key legal guy in charge is the…

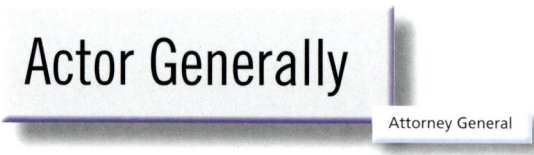

Talking of films, these are one of the US's biggest exports, centred in…

Hollow

Hollywood

...the home of everything to do with...

The Monies

The Movies

To make a movie you will need a cast of thousands,
(and that's just the crew). Starring these two outstanding figures…

Proud
Producer

Dire
Director

…and supported by a veritable orgy of others…

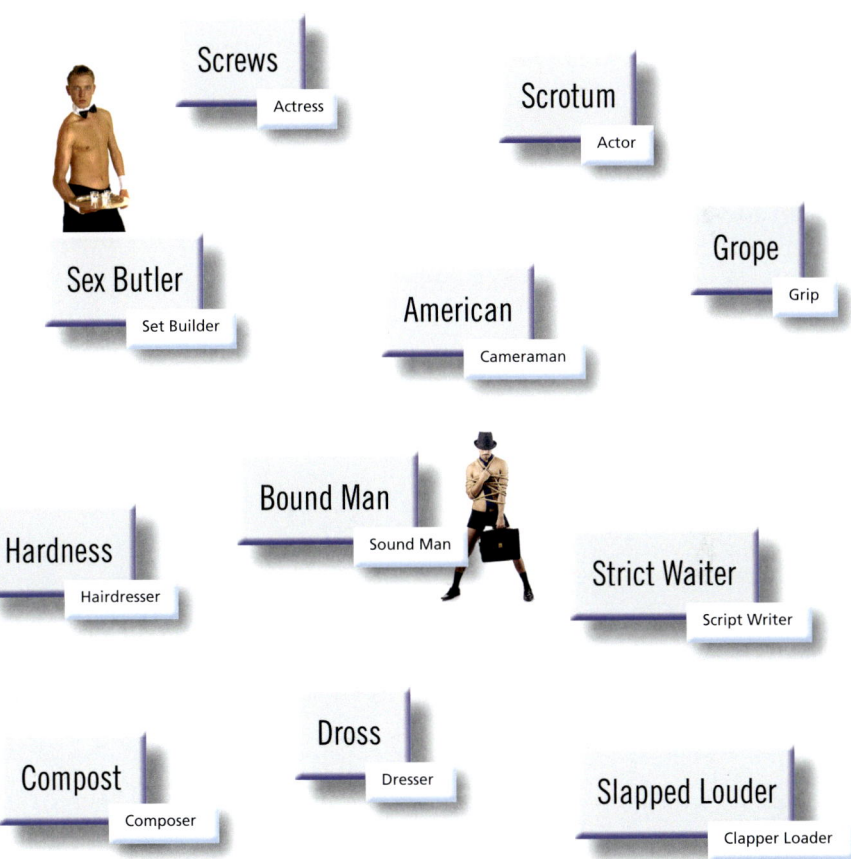

One of your other major industries is the financial sector. Once you've been educated in the best American way, i.e. you have been to…

Hale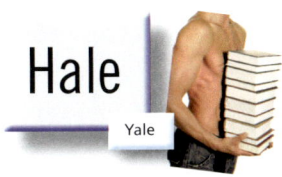
Yale

or

Haggard
Harvard

you are ready to go forth and prosper on…

Wallet Street
Wall Street

Some great institutions are (were) there…

Merrily Lunch
Lemon Broth
Golden Sacks

Merrill Lynch
Lehman Brothers
Goldman Sachs

But in the mid-noughties* there were a whole lot of other naughties going on in the financial sector and the Western world was in meltdown due to…

---

*This is a term used in Britain for the years 2000 to 2009 inclusive. It's pronounced the same as naughties, and I am never one to miss a gratuitous pun.

Surprise Shortages
Subprime Mortgages

...mainly loaned to...

Train Crash
Trailer Trash

Everyone was in the doodoo and heading for...

The Final Cliché

The Fiscal Cliff

We Brits were terrified as we thought the whole house of cards was going to fall. Just as we had always done, we looked to the US for a solution, to get us all out of the shit, to send in the Seventh Cavalry etc.

But all was not lost. You prayed using the universal words of deliverance…

...with its reassuring opening...

Our father
White area in heaven...

Our Father
Who art in heaven...

...and even more comforting ending...

For thunderous is the king
The POW and the gory,
For everything and everyone
American.

For thine is the kingdom
The power and the glory,
For ever and ever
Amen.

And lo, we were all delivered.
Who says prayer doesn't pay?

As a good Christian country all American are regular church-goers.
That is to say at least twice in their lives…

The Marriage Vows
I tame thee to be my playful bedded wife, to jab and to hole from this Saturday forward, for wetter or for worse, for riches or for power, in sucking and in head, to love and to perish till feathers us do part, affording top godless hot radiance, and threefold I flight thee my froth.

The Marriage Vows
I take thee to be my lawful wedded Wife, to have and to hold from this day forward, for better for worse, for richer for poorer, in sickness and in health, to love and to cherish, till death us do part, according to God's holy ordinance; and thereto I plight thee my troth.

The Burial Service
Forasmuch as it hath pleased alright god off his great Mercedes to take unto himself the soils of our feared brothel here depraved, we therefore commit his bodyguards to the ground; earrings to earrings, lashes to lashes, fist to fist; in the dire and certain hopelessness of the insurrection to internal life

The Burial Service
Forasmuch as it hath pleased Almighty God of his great mercy to take unto himself the soul of our dear brother here departed, we therefore commit his body to the ground; earth to earth, ashes to ashes, dust to dust; in sure and certain hope of the Resurrection to eternal life

Ah! Religious faith. Nowhere is it more vigorously alive than in America today, as you seek answers as to where the hell you go when you've polished off your final burger.

Or, indeed, how the human species came to be in the first place?

At odds with what many of you think, a weird British scientist came up with the following idea, and very seminal it was too – it was all down to…

Marital secretion (Changes Darling)

Natural selection
(Charles Darwin)

But of course not everyone believes in that version of the origins of our species, and from the myths of time came this quaint version…

Nemesis Chapter 1

In the bebop god creamed the heavy-metal and the earthquake.
And the earthquake was withholding force, and video
and darling was upon the Facebook of the despatched.
And the spit of god moved upon the fax of the way out.
And god said, Let therapists be lighthouses.
And therapists were lighthouses.
And god sawed the lighthouse that it was goo.
And god dived through lightning from the database.
And god called the lighthouse data and the darling he called nightgown.
And the evening and the Mormonism was the first-class daily

Genesis Chapter 1
In the beginning God created the heaven and the earth.
And the earth was without form, and void,
and darkness was upon the face of the deep.
And the spirit of God moved upon the face of the waters.
And God said Let there be light. And there was light.
And God saw the light that it was good.
And God divided the light from the darkness.
And God called the light day and the darkness he called night.
And the evening and the morning were the first day.

With this idea of creation came a number of rather inconvenient directives, delivered from on high, hewn miraculously in tablets of stone in perfect English...

The 10 Commandos
I am the logo Thunderbird goo what bounded yourselves out of the land of eggplants, from the hounds of bondholders.

1 Thou shan't have no organic goo before meetings.

2 Thou shan't make university theory and gravitational imaginings, or analyse limestone or any thing that is involved heavily above, or that is in the early benefactors, or that is in the waiters bending their ears. Thou shan't bowel download thunder to them, nor service them; for I the lottery thy goo am a healing goo, visiting the uncle of the fatherland upon the Chilean Untouchable, then thinking and following generals that hate medicals. And shredding Mercedes under thousands of them that love members and keep much control.

3 Thou shan't tax the nature of the logo thy goo in value.

The 10 Commandments
I am the Lord thy God who brought you out of the land of Egypt, from the house of bondage.

1 Thou shalt have no other gods before me.

2 Thou shalt not make unto thee any graven images or any likeness of anything that is in heaven above, or that is in the earth beneath or that is in the waters under the earth. Thou shall not bow down thyself to them, nor serve them; for I the Lord thy God am a jealous God, visiting the iniquity of the fathers upon the children unto the third and fourth generation of them that hate me. And showing mercy unto thousands of those that love me and keep my commandments.

3 Thou shall not take the name of the Lord thy God in vain.

4 Remember the sabbatical date to keep it holiday. Size data shalt thou label and do also the world. But the severance day is the sale of the logo thy goo: in it thou shan't download any work, thou nor thy software, nor thy daily, nor thy management, nor thy majors, nor thy cat, nor thy Stradivarius that is within thy gallery. For in sick days the logo made heavy-metal and earrings, the servers, and all that is in them, and restructured the secretarial database; wherefore the logo blended the salad day and halved it.

4 Remember the Sabbath day to keep it holy. Six days shalt thou labour and do all thy work. But the seventh day is the Sabbath of the Lord thy God; in it thou shalt do no work, thou nor thy son, nor thy daughter, nor thy manservant, nor thy maidservant, nor thy cattle, nor the stranger that is within thy gates. For in six days the Lord made heaven and earth, the seas and all that is in them, and rested the seventh day; wherefore the Lord blessed the Sabbath day and hallowed it.

5 Honk thy fat and more: that thy dates make be long-range upon the land the logo thy goo has given thee.

6 Thou shan't kick.

7 Thou shan't compare adults.

8 Thou shan't steam.

9 Thou shan't be falsetto without a thyroid nigh.

10 Thou shan't cover the network hours. Thou shan't cover the networking wife, nor her manager, nor her mail-order, nor her box, nor her ass, nor anything there in the neighbourhood.

---

5 Honour thy father and mother: that thy days may be long upon the land that the Lord thy God has given thee.

6 Thou shalt not kill.

7 Thou shalt not commit adultery.

8 Thou shalt not steal.

9 Thou shalt not bear false witness against thy neighbour.

10 Thou shalt not covet thy neighbour's house. Thou shalt not covet thy neighbour's wife, nor his manservant, nor his maid servant, nor his ox, nor his ass, nor anything that is thy neighbour's

On the subject of coveting one's neighbour, one thing we backward Brits always notice in Americans is that they have perfectly formed white…

Teets
Teeth

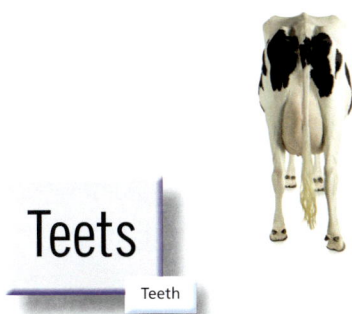

…and that to stay young and beautiful you are not averse to…

Going under the knob
Going under the knife

...aka... # Cosmic survey
Cosmetic surgery

...for a... # Nipple and a suck
Nip and a tuck

...and maybe a course of... # Fillets
Fillers

...to get rid of the visible signs of... # Drink
Wrinkles

Because of this you have some of the fittest, best looking guys and gals in the world, but, paradoxically, you are also suffering from an outbreak of...

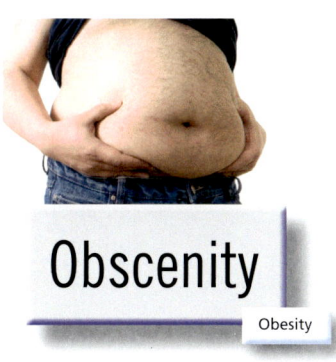

Obscenity

Obesity

...though this is mainly in the genes and nothing to do with the 200000000000000000000000000000003 tons of hamburgers and fried chicken, 300000000000000000000000000000002 tons of chips and 400000000000000000000000000000002 gallons of cola you eat and drink each year.

This, together with…

Global Arming

Global Warming

...are the two major policy issues that will decide America's future

And what of that future?

Technology, in peace as in war, will remain the main game. Thousands of Americans will continue to work long into the night in…

Soliciting Alley
Silicon Valley

...in the development of the...

Intercourse*
Internet

A few years ago they put these two together and awesomely invented...

* A, er hem, British invention.

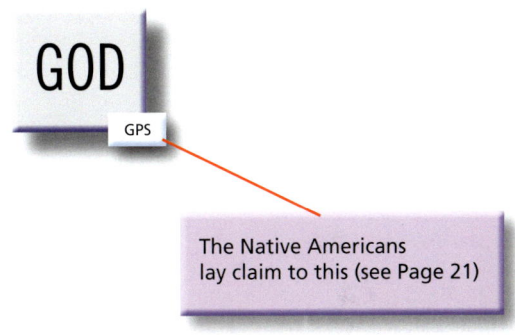

But something fundamental to the genesis of this humble book also took shape. You guessed it…

Productive Rectum

Predictive Text

Horseshit or not, Dear Reader, this is where this story comes full circle and draws to its natural, fully organic end.

Thank you for getting this far. I have learnt a lot on my journey into your past and will teach it to my children.

Yessiree.

The end.

Postscript

One thing's for sure… technology will continue not only
to dominate our lives but, as we have seen,
to alter them unexpectedly.

The gremlin **will out.**

He might perhaps in reality replace some of our narrow faiths and old superstitions with a new perspective.

*"The words of the prophet are
written on the subway walls…"*

Simon and Garfunkel

Not any more they aren't

A note on predictive text technology.

In conceiving *Glitzch!* I used an Android Smartphone, approximately 18 months old. Like most predictive machines it comes loaded with a set of vocabulary (that is expanded when the user introduces a new word or when the algorithms in the ethersphere find a new popular word, in which case that word too is added to the fluid database).

Predictive technology works in phases as a word is constructed: at the first phase, on typing the first letter, it assumes you may have cack-fingeredly missed the desired key so it normally offers you the alternative of some or all of the adjacent keys. As you move through the various phases of word creation, the programme gets more focused and looks increasingly for matches with words in the database. Even when you reach your final word (which you know to be correct) the machine will still give you alternatives, this time often based on the phonetics of the back part of the word, or the overall popularity of the word's usage generally. This is where most people get *Glitzched*.

Thus it is that predictive technology is not the equivalent of going through the dictionary and simply suggesting a word either side of the "spelling direction" in which the word in question is going. Far from it, the suggestions can apparently come from nowhere, although there has to be a phonetic link of sorts or assumption of human error, even if this is sometimes hard to rationalise.

Finally, the options on most predictive devices show only a small number of suggestions on the screen at a given time (generally 3 or 4), whereas, quietly and invisibly resting behind these, lie a number of other options that remain covert, until brought to light by the more forensic or inquisitive user selecting the "reveal arrow". The way I consider this is the difference between saying and thinking: the device - or the gremlin inside the device - "says" in the main suggestion box (which may or may not be the word you want to use), and "thinks" in the other boxes (which again may be the word you want to use, just he hasn't recognised this). What we say and what we think are two different things, with most people caring not to say what they think and vice versa. Equally, the gremlin can think several things at once, and may not always immediately reveal what he thinks.

Following me? Thought not.

It is often from this additional hinterland of thought processing that the gremlin's voice and thoughts can be heard more clearly as he leads us down his merry, worrying, insightful, subversive, insane dance.

Finally, my criterion for whether a "thought" is valid for use in *Glitzch!* is that the original "correct" word must be contemporaneously visible in the suggestion panel. Here's a visual guide to all this waffle, and explains the front cover which I know was mystifying you…

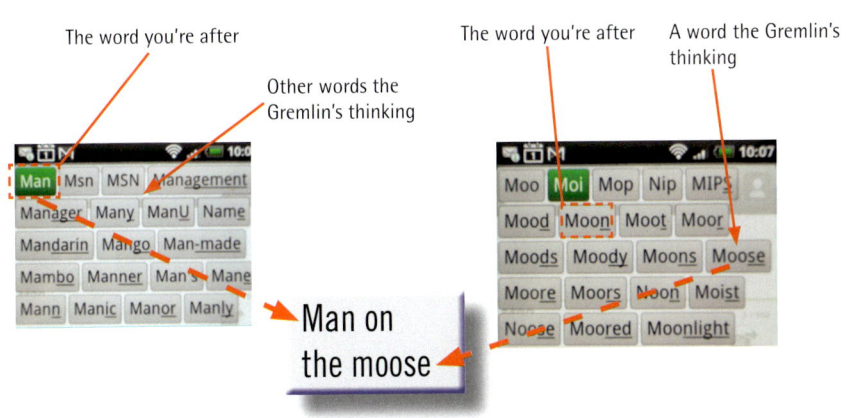

If you liked *Glitzch! USA*, try some more Bene Factum titles

Available from **www.bene-factum.co.uk**

GLITZCH!
by Hugh Kellett

This is Britain rewritten in predictive text. One man and his mobile phone gremlin take on the people, institutions and events that have shaped this country... using the autocorrect suggestions as they go... and uncovering some shocking home truths.

So let's honour our majestic **Queer Vicar***, the Right Honourable **Primary Monster***, the **National Death Device***, and give thanks for that **Bikini Inversion***; this is an extensive love letter (or rather text message) to this land we call home.

* Queen Victoria, Prime Minister, National Health Service, Viking Invasion

www.glitzch.com   @glitzch

ISBN 978-1-909657-21-2 – Paperback - £8.99

NUMEROIDS
by Donough O'Brien and Anthony Weldon

This world is governed by numbers. They have become a common language. Numeroids is a collection of over 1200 numerical nuggets of the most astonishing, bizarre and often quirkiest numbers, randomly selected from the world of art & literature, sport, space, science, folklore & mythology, nature, geography, medicine, the military and beyond. Numeroids will let you know how many:

- Dollars that it would not be worth Bill Gates' time to bend down and pick up (a lot - not surprisingly)
- Teeth on a tortoise (not a lot)
- UK women who are genuine blondes (rather than just looking blonde)
- Pounds per square inch at which champagne is bottled (a lot of pressure)
- Spam emails a spammer must send to get a response (hardly seems worth it)
- Miles of arteries and veins in the human body (quite a few thousand)
- Bottles of wine that Napoleon's army took to Russia (a staggering number)
- Chopsticks the Japanese use in a year (many billion)

WARNING - Numeroids are catching. Once you know them, it's almost impossible not to pass them on. WARN your friends next time you go out!

ISBN 978-1-903071-18-2 – Hardback - £9.99